To: N

G

A Journey of Discovering

God's Grace, Love, Mercy and Blessings

Expressed in Poetry

Freddie C. Taylor

In God we All Must Trust

2016

FT

Email: TaylorFreddie588@gmail.Com

Also on Amazon.Com

To Betty

God Did It!

A Journey of Discovering God's
Grace, Love, Mercy and Blessings
Expressed in Poetry

By

Minister Freddie Taylor

Forward

I was born on October 24, 1949, the oldest of twelve children, in a very small country town in Louisiana. I was raised in a broken home and never knew my earthly father. Don't look for the glamorous accolades of my life long achievements here. I was a juvenile delinquent and had no man to turn to for guidance, my life had been turned upside down. I was a high school drop-out at 17. At the publishing of this book, I am --- and I am blessed to be able to say, I'm saved now, and sanctified, I'm filled with the Holy Ghost, and I am still attending the University of Jesus Christ, majoring in Kneelogy!

I give my thanks to God for the wisdom and strength He has given me to share with you the deceptions of lies that have seduced my life for years; and to compose my life experiences in these spiritual truths. These inspirational words were first revealed to me (and me only) to understand. Then God's spirit spoke to me and said, "Write them in a book, make them plain and full of clarity, for the readers and for the hearers so that all men might know and understand the truth in this book."

As I traveled through life with notepads in my mind, sin dressed me up like a vagabond, had me running around high and drunk like a wayward man, homeless and lonely, living and eating out the trash can and moving me around from state to state. Sin had me searching for the dead man's path. Then, I incarcerated myself from jail to jail; ran in and out of drug rehab centers, trying to escape the wraths of God's wages. I wrote then, and am still writing about these experiences that have put a ton of weight upon the shoulders of my soul.

And if the truth be told, I lived a saved life for a moment, until sin took its occasion and again I found myself doing all sorts of ungodly things, in which were only stumbling blocks in many forms of deceptions. I forsook the right way to pursue the wrong things, until God, through the spirit of his Son Jesus, called me out to live Holy and gave me a new mind and a new heart.

In my distress, I cried out to God for his guidance and direction. And at that very moment, the Spirit led me to get a bus riding pass. As the bus approached a certain building, Temple of Faith Church Of God in Christ on 1550 Glenwood Avenue, Atlanta, Georgia, the Spirit said, "Get off this bus at the stop ahead." I cannot begin to tell you what the Holy Ghost did to and for me when I stepped into the building and into the truth.

Now it gives me great pleasure to introduce myself in this book and to be used for Christ. This book is a small glimpse of light, to share my experiences with the world, revealing the struggles I had with sin, and the goodness and mercy God showed me in my deliverance. What I can tell you is that I'm still rejoicing.

Yours Truly,

Minister Freddie C. Taylor

Acknowledgements

First I thank God, who is the head of my life. Who through His unmerited favor of grace and mercy, has allowed me in this time of my life, the pleasure to write this book; And now will I take this great opportunity to express my thanks, my gratitude, and my appreciation to all my friends and associates.

From the preachers standing in the pulpits, to the superior rated elite, I thank you for the role you have played in my life. I am extremely indebted to these individuals and I wish to acknowledge their unknowingly significant contributions of knowledge, their unquestionable insight and feedback, and their godly characters of profoundness.

To the individuals standing on the corners selling their souls, opinionated crackheads, homeless persons sleeping on the streets, I have learned from each of you even during the season of my life when I lived on the streets with you. All of these individuals and all of my experiences helped me to compose these essential elements of thoughts into this, my first book of poetry.

Great effort and genuine reflection have gone into these writings to assure that they are of the truth and are not just another quotation or story I have heard. These writings are from non-fictional experiences, through which I have lived in the past, and where I'm now living, in the Spirit, and in the knowledge of being truthful.

I truly thank God for putting all of you in my life, at this time of my age (for God's grace is sufficient), for stabilizing my life in His son Jesus, the Christ; who became the Father I never had. Thank you my Father, for being my God.

And now, as I continue with thoughts of appreciations for some very special people, who without a shadow of doubt, went through great lengths to assist me in completing the work of "God Who Did It". God knows I needed their awesome skills to help and direct me.

I truly thank my Pastor, Superintendent Thomas L. Frazier, for the unwavering belief and love he has shown to me, even when I lived on the streets and through all the phases in my life. I thank God for Evangelist Aaronetta Wright-Harris who in her own unique way, imbedded into me the "*want to*" and the mindful determination to complete this book. After several years of attempting to postpone and or give-up on writing this book, in came Dr. Valerie Bennett, who together, along with my beautiful wife, stood strong in motivation and continual encouragement, for with that, strengthened me and truly, I thank and praise God for them.

Finally, this last segment of thanks is so hard to write as I think about the challenges I have had in learning what it means to be good father. I thank God for my families, both past and present, but, especially to my children Mia, Mark, David (who has gone home), and Joseph, my youngest. To my lovely wife, Evangelist Betty G. Taylor, who would not, could not, and did not let these writings lay wasted, gathering dust in my mind. For these five also, have I written books of poetry in poems, that I pray will follow, "God Who Did It". There are just so many that have shown their love (Thank You) and you know who you are. As I write, I look into the eyes and hearts of each one of you and say with a pure mind, and my whole heart I say Thank you, Thank you, and Thank God for you.

Truly, I Love You All Very Much

Thank You.

Minister Freddie C. Taylor

Contents

1   God is' The Blesser of the Blessed

2   A little big lie

3   My sweet Betty boo (part 1)

4   Been there, done that

5   My way out

6   Time plus time

7   My Thoughts

8   The fight of my life

9   One hundred and eighty degrees turn around

10   Me

11   A Thief

12   Bad Feelings

13   Crazy Craving

14   The Truth

15   God can still save

16   God reconstructed my life

17   Jump starting my life

18   O' my God

19   The Hell Bound train (part 1)

20   What's going on, and what's up with that

21   My Pandora Box

22   "Know this" God won't leave you like He found you

23   A lake called wonderful waters

24   A real quick fix

25   Why am I here

26   Forgiven from a heart full of hell

27   A vision

28   During desert time

29   What some men don't do

30   Wanted, Dead or Alive

31   My sweet Betty boo (part 2)

32   What's going on and what's up with that

33   The Hell Bound Train (part 2)

34   A sinister Friend

35   The new man

36   It's all about Christ

37   O' hopeful thinker

38   The expectation of a dead man's path

39   A seed for thoughtful growth

40   Manifested Tendencies

41   Stoned

42   A Christ-must tale, Told

43   My Soul

44   How

45   Drugged by a dream

46   A Fathers love

47   Living in a storm

48   My storm story

49   Lord' Increase my faith

50   Total Control

51   My soul is afraid

52   The ungrateful

53   Stolen from a princess

54   God has restored me again

55   My Queen

56   When I was there

57   If walls could talk

58   O' my God

59   I must tell God

60   A wonderful, wonderful friend

God is, the Blesser of the Blessed

As I write about my darkness,

I was living on the streets,

sleeping on cardboard sheets.

Naked was I, cold and in perils,

down on my sick bed,

close to the chambers of death.

A storm came and the winds blew

And the waves rocked my mind.

Frighten and afraid,

I waited in faith and the miracle happen.

I looked up, and he filled my soul

With the Holy Ghost and joy

I am so glad

God did what God had done

He is done what he had doing

And he is doing what he had done,

what he said he would do.

And I thank and praise him

God is, The Blessed of the Blessed

A little big lie

A big little lie don't care who tell it

A bully he is, care only for himself.

But I am your friend, can you not see,

You would break my heart,

if you disclose poor me.

Close to my heart I keep my friends;

My enemies are sealed in my mind, I'll keep them closer.

But now that I have my life back,

And my enemy is trying to kill me.

But God is in control,

And God can't lie.

God want help, if you don't first try to help yourself.

And the true will set you free.

Actually, do something for yourself,

Come out from among them,

Try Christ, He will set you free from lies.

He will fix it,

And that's the absolute Truth.

God don't tell little big fat lies.

My Sweet, Sweet Betty Boo (part 1)

Betty Boo Where are you?

Mama here goes that women again,

She's doing what she does, just to be seen.

At night on my bed,

I dreams bout my boo.

I go into the streets, walking and running

Searching in darkness, listening for her footsteps

Smelling for her perfume I bought for myself.

O" Betty boo, my sweet, Betty boo,

Know you not I love you much".

And will melt a dead snail,

for messing with, my boo.

I have love one once,

or maybe twice.

God gave her to me,

And I made her my wife.

O" my sweet Betty boo

where are you?

Why are you not lying next to me?

Where are you, am I asleep"?

Been there done that

When I walked the streets of ungodliness

I looked for someone to blame.

I was a people pleaser, O, yes I was,

I suffered the pain of shame.

I remember the shame trapped in a snare,

like a fool to the correction of a jail.

I tried to deliver myself, my way,

a way that that leads to hell.

I have been there, done that,

the life of a way fairing man.

Couldn't find no peace

nowhere I laid,

neither could I find a friend.

I lived in the tombs with dead men,

that vexed my hearts at night.

But, in my lying ways, I sort the truth,

the truth about Jesus Christ.

Been there, doing the things I've done,

which drove me crazy at time.

So much more the word of God,

Which redeemed, my heart and mind.

I have been there, and done that,

all of that, but no more.

I'm saved by his blood.

My way out

I remember how hard I thought it was,

to fight my triggers against my fears

My trigger was money, money, money.

Money carried me to my entrapments,

like a bird trapped in a cage.

But God through the Holy Spirit

taught me positive thinking bring positive living, showed me a new way to life.

Jesus did not leave me like he found me.

Jesus was—My Way Out

Time plus Time

Sometime time,

time to a man is like kryptonite to his mind.

Time plus Time, equals Time.

It is God who control, time.

Man need to take time to make time to have time,

And press to fine time to give God time,

for worship and for praise.

It is now time, to make time, for study time,

time for fasting; its praying times.

Men even try to stealing time,

buying time and losing time.

Some are doing hard time in an evil times,

calling it time out and time in.

But God" always make and takes time,

when we are heartbroken,

to hear us in our sad and hurtful times.

We are living and missing the time,

killing and trying to tell time,

and time will not wait for no one.

God is controlling time, it is his,

and he's always on time.

So, Time Plus Time

Equal Gods time

All the time

My Thoughts

So------many thoughts are rambling through my mind;

Unstable they are, piercing holes,

Through my righteous brain;

They come and they go, I can't control,

and my imagination,

always plays a deceptive game;

Convincing me" my thoughts are holy-----wrong,

You're not in sin, right-----wrong;

No more sinful lies, right-----Wrong"

My thoughts demands I surrender to the powers of sin.

My thoughts are progressively stressfully,

wrong and ungodliness;

But these, my thoughts, I must resist,

And I know they will flee;

I give back the power wrong gave to me;

And surrender to the power of the Holy Ghost,

that will glide my thoughts,

to the righteousness of God,

through his son Jesus Christ-----Right,

And Now I'm saved, I Believe

The Fight of my life

O, king sin, I know, you train well for all your fights.

But tonight, your fight is with Christ;

Who'll fight for me to save my soul?

To keep me holy and whole;

It is he, you fight, for my life;

and against the truth you will not stand.

And tonight I stand with the word of God,

a saved and sanctified man.

Your truthful lies, sounded real good

your wicked ways, Insane"

Christ the righteous will fight for me

As I praise his holy name.

I confessed my sins long time ago,

I believe he was raised from the grave

I have no doubt; He'll knock you out;

and keep me holy and saved.

Now, your last contender was living in sin;

lost within his minds,

to believe, you were really a winner

So many men have fallen to you,

The wretch, the undone and the sinners;

So some, you beat to death, king sin,

and I know without a doubt;

If you give your life to Jesus Christ,

No doubt, he will bring you out.

180 degrees turnaround

I rent no space to negative thinking

my mind belongs to the Lord

Who turned me around, set me free

all through the power, of the mighty God.

I walk upright, not in uncertainty,

Christ changed my point of view.

I walk by faith now, not by sight,

I've turned, and I know he's true.

By his grace my life was saved,

Sin was making me doubt.

I shout hallelujah, praising the lord,

My heart really, cried out.

From the valleys of death, to the pulpit,

Sin had a hold on me,

But God, saw my heart was right,

Saved me and set me free.

God has turned, my life, all the way around,

So I can see nothing, but no one else, but Him.

"But, now I can see the SON shine"

Me

Me, I'm sticking with the Lord that loves me

He gave himself to save me;

And I'll stand, be who I am, and I'm Me.

In times past, I, me got myself in trouble;

And found myself alone, in lost vegas;

But, as for me, I really love him;

I really want to see myself saved, with me.

I pray with myself

and desire to see me change.

Always asking the Lord in prayer;

to have his way in our lives

in the name of Jesus, we pray.

Me, I have quickly learned to trust God,

That he is my refuge and strength,

He is a very present help,

when we are in trouble.

Me, myself and I, well;

Now we walk alone with Christ,

And we are all trying to get to heaven together,

Through Christ, I, myself, and Me.

A Thief

A thief comes to steal, kill and to destroy,

with thoughts of taking your life.

Your mind and soul, surely he want,

morning, noon and night.

He has no boundaries, he takes his time,

Considering everybody a prey;

And the things he does to convict your spirit

And steal your soul away.

My prayer time he put in his wallet

My will, he had in his sack.

My faithfulness that I had in God almighty;

He carried it on his back.

My life with Christ, he didn't desire,

Where Christ paid his blood and died;

Christ my refuge has stored me righteousness,

The thief couldn't live it if he tried.

Now, Christ lives here, and he's at home;

The thief left our house with nothing

Bad feeling

O, my God

On the outside:

I do acknowledge my spirit man,

on the inside.

I acknowledge the body,

you appointed to die.

Tell me O my Lord

Where shall my spirit search,

That I might find you,

And live again forever.

Good, but, very Bad spiritual feeling.

a man living without hope.

Marvelous is your work in creating me.

for my body to return to the ground,

where it was created and found, and,

The unknown expectations of death,

brings, very bad feelings.

O, my God

Crazy Cravings

I have some crazy cravings,

looking in the mirror at myself, saying;

This can't be a dream,

the plan God has for me, it's crazy,

God is so good I knew this wasn't a dream:

Then I remember the choices I made,

Picking up over and over, and over again;

The cravings, I could've been casting out;

It was crazy living in my crazy cravings.

Telling jokes and living lies,

just to die in them.

In the darkness of my crazy craving

Somehow I heard Gods speak to me.

Saying, "I will give you the zeal,

to seek my knowledge,

and a heart to cry for understanding".

I step back, took a deep breath, then step forward,

and realized who was my higher power.

Don't be amazed or surprised,

at my first step to recovery.

I made one step into the loving arms
of my Lord and Savior Jesus Christ.
Crazy- Cravings

The Truth

The truth; is him that created me.

In the spontaneous thoughts in the game of fame;

Comes with the expectations of living large;

Bring us to the end results, of lies,

which leads us far from, the Truth.

Come on somebody.

The Truth,

The Truth, don't tell no lies

I laid in shame once, without the truth,

convinced that sin would set me free.

In the mist of my troubles,

God made me a promise, but said,

"Mortify therefore your members

which are upon the earth;

Stand still and see

Who it is,

that has set you free".

The Truth,

The Truth came, and brought you back,

back to your life with Him.

So,

I thank God

For my Lord and Savior, Jesus Christ.

God Can Still Save

I was born a bastard had lots of kin;

struggled with Christ, and lived in sin.

A covetous man, didn't have no rules;

a wayward man, didn't know no school.

A pagan man who wouldn't believe,

That God would supply my every need.

When I needed my friends, they couldn't help,

then God taught me, how to love myself.

God open my eyes that I may see,

not to doubt the Christ that lives in me.

Today I live, not for myself,

as one, who walks by faith.

I now keep His commandments,

to do his will?

O God, I love your way.

God has made me a living proof

That He can still save…

God has restored me again

My cracked-up life was sinful and wrong,

living for ungodliness all day long.

Restore my soul O' Lord, with my head hung low.

I have nowhere to run, and nowhere to go.

Can't escape this trap I've tried all night.

Have no one to turn to, and no strength to fight.

I've prayed and I've prayed,

God, please wash away my sins.

I've received and understand,

that Christ was my friend.

Lord forgive me, against you I have sinned.

I believe you can, please restore me again.

He has restored me, 'all His people, and gave me life,

and made my life to shine.

I now walk by faith, not by sight,

Renewed, with a very sound mind;

Thank you, Lord, You've restored my state.

Of body and mind to a brand new faith.

God, you have restored me again"

Jump starting my life

I was stranded in sin, and asked, will someone help me?

And there was no one.

I tried to walk that 12 step ways, they say that works;

I stood on the principles they had,

But these affirmations made it worse.

However, in the mountain of my mind,

My thoughts daily was as, if I'm dying.

And all their traditions of happiness, taught to me.

Made me to see, I was looking in all the wrong places,

With a guiding light, I looked,

In another world, I looked,

I even searched for tomorrow, with one life to live.

And at night, I walked around with the young and restless'

I also tried the bold and the beautiful.

But in the edge of the night,

I beheld my foolishness laughing at my miseries.

Until repentance showed up, pricking my heart;

God's forgiveness, came down from heaven,

like a mighty rushing wind, breathing out fire.

That's all was needed, to Jump Starting my life.

O' my God, I Pray

O' my God

In my weakness, strength me;

With your strength make me strong.

O' my God, I am weak and need you.

Down in my transgressions, a sinners state

I do realize, "I need you."

To forgive my sins, and my unrighteous doings;

Please remove them, from before your eyes.

Help me, O' Lord, to stand in your righteousness;

"I Pray"

O' my Lord

Make better your people,

Make better your people O' my Lord.

Let our prayers become our praise.

Let us gloried your holy name

Teach us to know knowledge;

That it will lead us to more understandings.

That it will keep us saved, sanctified,

 filled with the Holy Ghost, Your Spirit.

"I Pray"

Now, O' my God

Make better my weakness, and stronger my strengths

Then, make space for the talent you given me,

and keep me.

"Truly, I Pray"

The Hell Bound Train #1

There was a man who never drank before,

the man started drinking, till he couldn't drink anymore.

He felt asleep, with a troubled brain'

 dreamed he was riding this hell bound train.

Thcy had ample fuel they were shoveling bones,

and the engine sounded like a thousand groans.

Inside the trains sit virgin devils,

the headlight of the train was like a gravestone banner.

We heard then, the conductor yells,

the devil himself is the engineer.

Then, the train sped up through an awful cave,

while sulfuring fumes burn their hands and face.

Then the lightning flashed, the thunder roared,

it shook and rattle those on board.

Passengers were of a familiar crew, church men, gamblers, liars too'

red men, yellow men, black and white, they were all chained together, it was a terrible sight.

But the train sped on at a break neck speed,

on rails of vanity, jealous, lust and greed.

Then we heard the conductor yell, sinner man"

your next stop is hell.

Then, all the passengers begin to scream,

But, fame was begging the devil to please stop this train.

The devil looked at fame, and laughed, and said'

you have been living in greed,

you have marked and scorned people misery.

And after I brought you a shiny new rolls- Royce",

You said you were going, to the end of my road.

But, you worried the weak, you cheated the poor,

you marked their God with your hell bound pride.

And this time I will not lie,

I'm going to land you in the lake of fire.

where your flesh will burn with flames that roar,

and away from hell there is no door.

Soon, that drunk man woke up with a sweating cry,

his clothe were wrinkle, and his hair stood high.

and prayed as never before in that hour,

O' Lord' deliver me from the devil's power.

His prayer of faith, were not in vain, he accepted Christ, and eternal life was gained.

What's going on and what up with that (part 1)

O, brothers, O, sisters, O, sisters and O, my brothers

Tell me, what's going on and, what up with that?

What're we going do bout,

this generation gap of crack babies?

Shall we vote'em in to be governors and senators?

But where will we find relief? R-E-P-E-N-T-A-N-C-E!

Times are getting hard, well they're gonna to get harder,

Gas going up, so is drugs,

Men building bigger jails with smaller cell,

some men dealing, some men dealing,

and the food stamp line getting longer.

How long are we gonna take this;

Destroying our bodies along with our souls,

And our evil imagination,

Is carrying us away like a bird,

To destruction "never again to return and have life.

But who bewitched you, that you believe not the truth?

Disobedience and pride,

Which are only emotions out of control?

That in the which, the invisible powers of darkness enslave.

Brothers and sisters

Be not proud of your evil portion of this life.

But turn, before, the real light make it darker,

And you find death.

Now, that's what's going on, and that's what up with that.

The Pandora's Box of God

In my hour of prayer,

The Spirit of God came, and spoke with me;

Unman and shaken,

At the four kind of horrible things, I seen;

Waiting to be released, for the disobedience of men;

For they cried out warning men spirit'

of the unanticipated things' coming;

That their punishment lingers not, it's here;

I found myself in weakness willing to obey.

And the spirit carried me up'

And immediately, I looked;

And saw thousands, being eliminate, by the sword;

And the dogs tearing them apart;

Along with the fowls of the heaven, and the beast of the earth;

Destroying and devouring them; O' what a sight;

I prayed, and I was not afraid, they also were warned.

But again I looked,

And I saw, the most horrible thing, never seen before;

Thousands of thousands, of thousands "Dead Men";

Not able to participate in the resurrection of Jesus Christ,

Running and screaming and mourning and crying'

And so being repaid;

Men dead bones I saw, dried up, and so given up;

They were dead in the affliction of ungodliness;

Destruction is their punishments sent to men.

So if, and when you get one, Pray;

For what's becoming, upon the souls of men;

From the Pandora's box of God.

Know This, God won't leave you like He found you

I was cold, sleeping on the bricks,

Covered with cardboard sheets;

I asked myself;

Are you seeking God?

Or, are you seeking for God, to find you?

I was a foolish, void of understanding'

Couldn't perceive, wouldn't believe;

And neither would I try, to cry-out;

Running around in the mountains of my mind;

Living with a thousand of thousands of thousands, dead men'

in tombs, crying and cutting myself with stones.

But I knew in my heart

if I could just see Jesus,

He want leave me where he found me.

I was trapped in a cage like a bird, with no one to help

and did not know, I was living with the lost, In Vegas,

"And, that is, for my life".

But I knew, Right away

Jesus wouldn't leave me, sleeping on them bricks,

Jesus wouldn't leave, me, under those cardboard sheets.

Jesus wouldn't leave me; in a cage like a bird.

Sleeping in pain covered in shame, having nothing to eat.

But when I started to believe, I'll tell ya

God did not leave me, like He found me.

And I'll say to you

He won't leave you, where you are, "either".

A Lake called Wonderful Waters!!!!

Where are we now, my lover and I?

We are going down,

In the waters called wonderful.

Swimming with the adulterous

While tanning with the fornicators, and,

we are all, skinny dipping in darkness.

My lover knew' it was wrong for me,

to swim in these sin filled waters;

In the which' I was not familiar with;

For daily, these strong currents,

persuades me, to enjoy these ungodly waters of life;

Around the corner;

Down in, one of the deepest part, he said,

Just look at this beautiful' death taking scenery;

Where there are vast numbers of sinful lives.

waiting in his shinning life of lies;

Beholding my humbleness of holiness;

Finally, in one of the most deepest part,

Came waves, of lustful pleasures, parading themselves,

took, by breath away.

My heart was beating out of control;

My body became paralyzed, turning cold and blue.

And, with my last breath, and, in pity,

I turn to my lover, and ask.

Where are you, and,

What is this, you have done?

O' no, I said to myself, my life, is no more;

My lover words deceived me;

And drown me, in the lies of his tears.

And I found myself, smoking, in the lake,

That burning with FIRE, in

The Lake called Wonderful Waters!!!!

A Real Quick Fix

Yes. When you become friends with sin,

It's like a quick fix, very fast and smooth;

He guides you, the way of sinners

Listen my brothers, sinners and all'

In a quick fix, there's plenty of ways to fall,

Respect yourself; listen to the Spirit of God;

And, when the hook-up comes,

Pull the cotton out your ears,

put it in your mouth;

Listen again, my brothers and sisters,

You can change your behaviors,

before you can't break them!

And never do this

Run to a mile, where you can't, walk back.

And, The Real Quick Fix is

Let Christ run your life for you;

And don't worry about running back, to sin.

Respect yourself, by respecting others;

Keep the love, God gave to you, by giving it away.

This is "A Real Quick Fix. JESUS for your life"

Why am I Here?

Why am I here, I asked myself?

Why no man would claim me' and,

Who it was that made, or, that had begotten me.

But, they all knew, just how I became,

Some said it was done, through an unnamed man.

Who am I? Well, I know no earthly father

I had no wonderful Dad.

My grandfather was the father to be;

And 'a lover I never had'.

I remember being there, stuck in the mud,

Sinfully mad, shamefully sad.

But. Why am I here?

Because, I was there;

In riotous living of confusion;

That drove me here' so I could see;

That' God himself had a plan for me.

That it was him' along" that had begotten me,

And his wonderful love, that had set me free.

The Question is "why am I here?

And The Answer is, to, "Why-I-am-Here?"

It's, So God can save me.

Forgiven From A Heart full of Hell

I was a menace of society, by hurting myself.

Cursing all day and lying all night;

Arguing in the church house'

And always ready for a fight.

While living with a heart full of hell;

I was unhappy and sad, angry and mad.

Lie at the altar, and treat my brother bad'

Saying I love God, whom I have not seen.

Why do I do these things, that I really don't mean

At this stage of my life'

I call common sense' a super power.

And, at the spur of that moment' my confession was uttered

Repentance came fast, and deliverance set me free.

From a heart full of Hell

A Vision

As I prayed, in my hour of prayer,

I saw a vision that came out of nowhere.

Clothed like a man, riding on a white horse,

Spoke with me' And said,

Cush, the son of Cannon

an Ethiopian' is a black man.

And no, he cannot change his skin.

Now stop' trying to make, the faith of God

to no effect, with your doubtfulness.

Had not God brought you

from the shame of being resented and neglected,

unto true repentance.

But traps, are in your way

and stumbling blocks, were placed before you.

Stand still said the Lord, I will remove them all.

Said the spirit, that sat upon the horse

For you will be filled the more, with his spirit,

and you shall, be filled;

With the fire of love, joy, peace and praise.

Now go' and tell what's in your heart.

Tell what great things God has, and is doing, for you.

Bring forth fruit to repentance.

Then the spirit, dressed in man clothes,

That came from God, left me.

Doing Desert Times

When you are quiet and still,

When you are in an empty and dry land,

That some call 'their closet'.

'God himself' will speak to you.

When you give Christ your time' to talk with him

it brings you great rewards;

When you are hungry and thirsty for righteousness

and spending quality time, in desert time.

He will fill you with his goodness.

When you are along and have no hope

He will satisfy your longing soul;

He will fill you with so much joy.

When you are doing desert time

God can mold and shape you into a vessel

that will always shine in darkness.

In desert time, God has a unique way,

of bringing you closer to him.

To walk and talk with you;

And to exercise, your body and mind,

your soul, and your spirit;

Put a pin in this: In God through Christ,

I'm no longer dancing with the devil.

Desert Time is quality time

Set aside, for you and the Master.

What? Some men don't know

What? Some men don't know?

That, the kibbles of tithes, and bits offering,

we offer to God, is sinful.

What? Some men really don't know;

Getting high on sin is a race to the gate,

And will fail to hear, the trumpet when it sounds.

I was twenty-two years old

when I knew the walk of sin;

No real chance, no real opportunity,

Only to stand in stupidity;

Now I found out that, some men (like me) didn't know,

that their Christian character,

is always on displayed by the Holy Ghost.

Tell me, what? some men don't know.

The good things God has for them that love Him,

And keep His commandments.

Wanted: "Dead or Alive"

Wanted: Ungodly dead men, who need Christ;

who's living an ungodly life;

Murders you are, whoever you are,

with shotguns of unwillingness, dying to comply.

Killing each other, robbing each other

for years and months and days.

In violent directions, you search for life.

only to find, dark emotional, ungodly pathways.

Through unclean spirits, you'll find horrible things...

So, who are these, masked men, coming in?

Carrying a sealed conscience, with swords of blood,

With weapons of jealousy, hater's for love.

With hot irons of madness they fight the truth

and, if they fight against God, then, what about you;

While they live among us, here in this 21st century; ha

Where women are falling in love with (outlaws), bad boys

and men worshipping their images made by hands,

and their minds, being carried away to destruction, in
corruption;

While, loving to live, to dance with the devil;

Their sons and daughters, (in the meanwhile)

Engaging themselves in killing, one another with the same;

These men are:

"WANTED: Dead or Alive"

For their non-faithful acts, of thinking to escape;

Fugitives they are, and running, from the law of the Lord.

Where they dare not, love their neighbors, as thyself,

Nor will they hate their lustful pride;

but will wallow in the muddy waters of desire for them.

But, when men hide themselves in the knowledge of the Lord,

they find their desires resting deep, in the living God.

WANTED

Outlaws running from the Word of The Lord

"There is a REWARD"

Eternal life: $0.00

My Sweet, Sweet Betty Boo (part 2)

I can't find you, where are you

My sweet Betty boo?

Finally she appeared, stepping like a whirlwind,

loving me in every which away, just for me.

But which way did she go?

Like a breeze through the door,

With a smile, and I caught that.

She made me dream about happiness again,

Comprehend?

And I caught that.

Is Betty boo gone wild?

And yes I got that…

Betty boo I love you much

In the sunshine, or in the rain,

in trouble days and through the pains.

Now I need to walk through the door.

Yes I will.

I love you much more…

What's going on and what up with that (part 2)

O, Sisters, O, brothers, O brothers and O sisters

Again, What's going on and what up with that?

How is it in the desperation of time,

life is bringing us to violence.

And how the devil bewitching some to believe in his lies.

How in a thirteen second good time, in a twenty-four hour world,

has women molesting boys and men raping girls.

Evil lustful men, and women, wrapped in their disguise.

Living in the same tomb, trapped in sinful pride.

Now the expiration of time, bring us to violence.

Men running to the suburbs, and running from the city;

The homeless in the trash can, the rich showing no pity.

They're sleeping on the outside,

The shelters are really truly packed.

You'll find no room in a county jail cell,

where the population there is mostly black.

And where do we find relief from babies smoking crack.

R-E-P-E-N-T-A-N-C-E

Now, that's what's going on, and that's what up with that

The Hell Bound Train (part 2)

The hell bound train was hordiculous, to me;

Seducing me to places I didn't want to be,

Showing me bad things, I didn't want to see;

I thank God, for putting, his hands on me.

As God pull me from the train,

I heard the conductor yell,

Five more minutes, we'll be home in hell;

There's one more stop, called, the praying hole;

Your very last chance, to pray, for your soul;

We just passed a sign painted in red

Saying' get off this train, at the stop ahead.

Then, I remember the scene, on the train last night,

Where the gambling church men, had begun to fight.

Passengers started screaming "What must we do?

To save ourselves, and walk like you do?"

Repentance, I said, believe in Christ,

The only way out, to save your own life.

But daily, I still watch that train,

Speeding up and down those tracks;

Full of men's souls that want to turn back;

I thank God through our Lord Jesus Christ

That, you put your hands on me.

A Sinister Friend

A wild flagitious friend, you are,

With the disastrous pains, you cause.

We were old friends, from yester-years,

Why we're not friends today.

You're used to cherished holiness, every day,

you walked, in a righteous state.

But, for all the evil, you are doing,

your friends are walking away.

They confront you, with love and kindness

You work them' with your thoughts.

Your sins will always remain with you,

when you make your friends your faults.

Treacherous and mysteriously, you are;

O' how ungodly your life must be;

But your "Hor-dic-u-lous favor"

That's coming from God

It's coming just wait, you'll see…

Tell Me Now "Why are you standing on my left side?"

No no no!

The New Man

In the trails of my faith

through the strength of God.

As I walked on the wild side,

my old man stood' in control.

Daily I struggled in my will of hearts,

Living the wickedness of lies, killing myself;

But 'The New Man' made up his mind.

And cried out, from the depths of his soul,

from his broken and contrived heart.

God heard him;

Washed and renewed him,

and delivered him, 'The New Man'

---- to Christ.

It's all about Christ

Some have sold their soul for fool gold,

But, it's all about Christ

Doing their business in destructive ways;

Wake up souls that cherish that gold;

Do you not know; It's all about Christ.

But, your souls will burn in the fire.

His name is Jesus, last name Christ,

It's all about Him, that will bring you peace,

In the middle of your storm

He will give you courage.

It's all about Him who will heal your body

And your mind in this evil time, like these.

It's all about Christ.

When you're confused and frustrated,

He will give you strength.

When in frustrations and discombobulating

He will show you, the peace in love,

that passes all understanding.

It's all about Christ

And yes God will give you hope

Yes God will redeem man back to Him, but

It's all about Christ.

O' Hopeful Thinker

O' Come with me, O' hopeful Thinkers

Your name has come up before God.

He has sent me to speak with you;

Because you have resolved your conflict

Without waiver nor doubt;

For this God has restored your name,

O' hopeful thinker

in your hope, of being with Christ.

For you did not wish for silver and gold

to feed the roots of evil;

But, knowledge and faith

to serve the Lord our God

for the hope of eternal life.

My hopeful thinking,

is rooted and grounded

in going back with Christ when He returns.

I am a Hopeful Thinker

The Expectations of a Dead Man

Men live the life, and die the death.

Some men are dead, walking right here, on earth.

And one of their expectations in sinful living,

is they will not, have to pay, for the life they live.

People who's not afraid of the judgment;

Neither do they expect, to swim, in the lake called fire;

They desire to be leaders of the blind;

and know not the way.

Teachers of righteousness living on, wrong-way avenue.

(swimming in the lake themselves)

 Dead men who expects the S-O-N,

to shine on them, with goodness and mercy.

While they stabilized, themselves, in tombs of ungodliness,

drowning, and cannot, cry-out:

But here again. The expectations of this here, dead man,

Is to seek, to be free, from the sins that's besetting,

and waiver's not at the promises of God.

Saying to the Lord' I confess with my mouth

You are my Lord, and Savior, the Christ in my life

And believe in my heart,

that God raised you, from the dead.

Now "The expectations of this dead man's life; Is Eternal life" with Jesus The Christ.

A Seed for thoughtful growth

The thoughts of a proud spirit,

the heart cannot humble.

Righteousness is restrained, knowing it's wrong.

But, here's a new song that I sing.

Not my will O' Lord, but thou will, be done in my life

If you wait on the Lord,

he will send you a comforting keeper;

to keep, and seal you, and never be the same again.

Now here's a seed for thought; Can you believe?

Some men are so dignified, and they can't live sanctified.

There are some that read the 66, of the king James,

Then, create a 67, in their own bible name.

Calling the book, Mine: the first charter: verses; one, two and three.

But then, God said to me, "Go

Be not afraid of their faces.

I have made your face like a flint:

Don't mix your fears and doubt;

You will only find confusion.

But, let's think on these things;

And be about praying about that"

Then give it to GOD, and let Him bless you.

PS. I really hope this helps.

Manifested Tendencies

God stands and God will knock;

Saying you have ears to hear' the eyes to see'

but have not, the heart to understand;

That, it would have been better,

not to have known God's righteousness,

then, to show your faith, dancing with another.

In the twilight, on a cold, and dark night,

not knowing, My son, that it was for your life.

God, sees my direction,

He knows, what it is, that I need,

So, in the manifestation of my mercy,

In the tenderness of my love

In the knowledge of my graceful word,

He shows me, the way to go.

Then I- just- couldn't live sinful, anymore.

His graceful word pierced my heart,

And his tender love was very effective.

I found repentance and forgiveness

in the manifestations of his mercy.

For it took longer for me, to repent,

than for The Lord Jesus Christ, to forgive.

Now, my tendencies are manifested in Holy living.

Stoned

As my tears begin to run down my face;

Like a river of water running over, a waterfall;

My thoughts were so, and overwhelming,

My expectations in life, were stopped cold'

in my what, when, where and how's.

I was drowning in the rivers of life, without Christ;

Crying and cutting myself, with stones

Going down real fast, living in sin;

I heard Him when he called, my name.

Saying I have forgiven you,

I have taken your place;

I- love- you- very much.

And, I will show you marvelous things;

You will not die, you- shall- live.

You shall be filled with my Spirit,

and shall be filled, again, the second time.

I realized then, I had been stoned,

right from the very start.

I am broken now; "Been set free".

A Christ-Must Tale' Told

Now, it was the day before Christmas, everything seems fine,

Men celebrating this holiday, having a good time;

At the blinking of an eye, things got out of hand.

Forgot about God, started celebrating with man.

It was the night before Christmas, when all through my house,

We prayed in our bedroom, for both me, and my spouse.

We don't believe in the Santa, people call, Mr. Claus.

We believe in the Son of God, who died on the cross.

Therefore, tomorrow we celebrate; God's son, being born,

We'll celebrate his birth, singing praises, hymns and songs,

But in that night, before Christmas, as quiet as could be,

No phones were ringing, everyone fast asleep.

I turned over in bed, and held my wife tight.

Could not wait for tomorrow, nor sleep, through the night.

On the morning, called Christmas, wasn't looking for no toy'

We were just glad to be alive, with Christ-must joy.

We kissed and hugged, then begin our day.

We got down on our knees and again, we begin to pray.

Now, our next door neighbors had cymbals and drums;

They played a new song, on their shiny new horn;

We celebrate not this day, in a holiday maze,

with Santa the Claus, the world has made.

I tell you a tale' don't be no-body's fool;

Don't shop in the daylight, where deception is the rule.

Today is bout, "Jesus (who was born of a virgin)",

That the world calls, Christmas day;

But, before he died, he gave us a command,

to walk, in his Christ-must way.

And, another tale I found, that were O' so true.

Today is the day Salvation was born,

to save both me, and YOU.

My Soul

Crying, as I lay here under this bridge

A listening, to the rain a falling;

This is the night; I lay down my pipe,

And pick up, the God given truth.

Even though, I thought knew God

I said to my soul, Did I make myself this way?

Then, My Soul spoke to my soul, saying;

You, young man "You Must Surely Die".

For the very first time, my soul cried-out;

Calling on the name of Jesus,

And I died and my soul came alive.

He saved me that night, under that bridge,

My soul was saved, my, My Soul.

How can a God so love, a sinner like me?

Through my ups and downs, my highs and lows,

my soul cried-out, and I was aware of my holiness.

The experiences under that bridge were very supernatural.

Up under that bridge "God lifted me up",

and my foot started stumping,

and my hands started clapping.

My lips started moving, and my tongue started talking;

Up under that bridge,

I looked and noticed, A change, had come over my soul;

The rain was a fallin', y'all, "the rain" the rain kept on falling

The rain, is still a fallin' deep down in, my Soul.

How

So, how do men override the voluptuous powers of sin?

Is it not, by turning to the word of God

That's leads us through temptations?

O' how do you not use, your God given powers

to rebuke the rage of the devil?

Is it not by the biblical words of intelligent?

Your faith in action; you doing the right things,

Your love for your brother's brother,

Your love of living for Christ;

O' How did I black-out, or, how did I denied?

My Lord Jesus Christ;

Who brought me out, of a horrible pit?

Who gave me eyes to see?

Who turned me from, that sinful place?

Who hung on the cross for me?

Who gave me the strength to walk upright?

Who promised, if I would live for him,

"I would inherit Eternal Life".

Teach me O' Lord, to use this power you gave to me,

to rebuke the thoughts of ungodly truths.

These voluptuous thoughts

I send them back; from which they came "To hell".

And Lord, Please, show me to live Holy.

I give up on the How.

Drugged by a Dream

I was drugged, and now I'm tripping, and, sin is at fault;

Dreaming horrible things, calling them, delightful things;

"This here dream" Tricked me "by captivating my thoughts".

Where I could not comprehend, and was drunk on a sinful delight;

Where, there were a legion of thoughtful pleasures.

Parading and appealing themselves, on pillow of desires.

And the why's "I was being drugged, on this dream about sin?

(sigh) The thunder and lightning started pounding my heart;

The storms of water overflowed my thoughts, convincing my mind.

Stop it" Stop these aren't my thoughts, and these, are not my dreams.

These dirty dreams in thoughtful details; do not belong to me;

Now, the last dream that came by, that day, was sin itself.

I immediately pressed, Pray. And said

Please my Lord", lock these made-up insane demoniacs spirits;

away in never-ever-land to never-ever be heard of again.

Calling out to Jesus, which I realized is my help.

God drugged me then with a Heavenly dream.

Spiritually

A Father's Love

A father will always express his love,

in ways, of giving himself over to care,

even, from the first day of his child's birth.

A father's love, will cherish his creation,

He will teach the wisdom of his life,

against the gods of this world.

He will give his knowledge

with deep compassion of awareness;

And he will reward his creation with good'

and correct him when they are not.

A father will stop the pain, that's out of control.

A father will die to see his creation grow.

When it's sunny and hot, a father is there?

When it's cold and they are hungry and thirsty

Even then, a father' will be there;

When his creation stumbles and falls,

A father (with tears in my eyes) will be there,

pick them up dust them off, and stand them up again.

A real father, will teach his son, to be a man,

and instruct his daughter to be a young lady to a woman.

A Father's Love will teach them to pray

and walk as they have been taught.

Thank God for A Father's Love…

Living in a Storm

When evil winds are blowing discords,

that brings destruction into your life;

When the thunder is roaring (like a lion) troubling ya,

and the lighting is flashing, making ya afraid;

Beware of the evil wind and the waters this life;

For they will come up fast to overtake you,

in the depths of your disappointments;

Yes they will carry you away, into their darkness;

But God, will cover ya with his righteousness;

The Lord will calm- your- storm,

and diminish the evil thoughts that's carrying you away.

He will shield you from, the electrical discharges

of this untoward generation;

He will make your storm to obey his every word

"If you really believe".

Then, and only then will you be safe in the tabernacle of God;

Sin will not carry you away in the endeavors of this life;

God will be your deliver, from the storms in your life.

Selah (Forever)

My Storm Story

I must give attention to the storms in my life.

and not to build my house upon,

a sandy foundation of unbelief

neither build a roof, of sorrowful straws of doubts.

But my spirit prays, for a solid foundation,

an insulated pavilion of the all mighty God.

So when the lightening flashes her eyes,

and the thunder speaks his husky voice.

God is there.

When the wind brings its cold and rainy disturbances,

and O' yes when the storms of lies appear,

in the whispering winds, with discords' clapping their hands.

My heart cries-out, "Help me O' Lord",

God is there.

God will pull you out of the rainy, windy storm

and set your feet on a solid foundation of truth.

Upon a rock against the gates of hell;

And God will be there.

When the storms fearlessly rage in your life,

to break down your will, and try to prevail

God will be right there.

To rebuke your storm and they will have obeyed;

To rebuke the winds, and they will have complied'

and the rains will stop falling, on every side.

Then the overflowing problem, you might have left,

in time, they will vanish and recede, all by themselves.

This is because, you trust in God…."

during your storm….

Lord' Increase My Faith

As I take my walk alongside the Lord to understand.

He said, Hear my son

Take the cotton out of your ears'

And put it into my mouth, to listen.

I will put my spirit into your heart

So, you can hear me, when I knock;

So, that you can hear me, when I speak,

So, that you will open the door to your heart;

So, that I may come in, and lead you to all truths.

So, that you may inherit your inheritance…

So that, Knowledge will be your strong tower;

An Understanding, you shall surely comprehend;

So that, these will show you, your increase of faith.

And the Wisdom, that makes one rich.

Now I understand, when you walk and talk with the Lord;

And, you open your heart, your situations changes;

The things you use to do, you don't do them no more;

I let, the dones be done

I walk with the Lord' NOW

And The Lord has increased my Faith.

God is, The Blesser

That's what I said

and The Lord' increased my faith

Total Control

Then God said, O' Man, put away the evil of your doings,

from before my eyes.

You know what it is when you're doing drive-bys,

and you're lifting up your name in fame

And you do the same thing, when you taking God glory

that you're bound, and on that, hell bound train.

O' Man, O' Man

Do you really, really think you can take control?

When you put God's name on blast?'

When you're spreading all kinds of fads?

When you putting God's word on sale?

When you're raising all mounts of hell?

What do you think, Tell me O, Man?

(When you're on your way to Hell)

When you're lying and cursing like a man,

(On your way to Hell)

Frying and popping like fatback in a frying pan?

Tell Me O' Man

How can you think, you can save yourself?

(Yelling you can make a dollar holla),

in your attempt, to buy you a ticket to heaven;

Are you out of control, O' sinful man?

When you find no strength for repentance,

And, you see no signs of deliverance;

In believing the words of the prophet;

To confess with my mouth "The Lord Jesus Christ",

And I believeth in thy heart

that God raise him, from the dead;

Now tell me O' Man, are you really in total control;

When you refuse to let the word of God fall into your heart;

To become a living testimony, of, true repentance;

Tell me, O' my man "Do you know what it is?

To let God have Total Control of your life, Today"

My Soul was Afraid

While living in these last times, watching today's horrors

I feared the scenes of sad tomorrows.

I observe the contempt of evil men.

How they fight against God committing their sins.

And I was lost in this world, and my soul was afraid.

Diligently, with my heart I searched, until I found repentance.

Deliverance was there, standing me up.

And, I heard God's voice saying, "Sin no more.

Yes, my soul was afraid".

I was afraid of that darkness, where I came from.

Where men are disguised, surrounded by friends;

Wearing a two-piece smile, with an ungodly new grin;

I tell you my soul is afraid for today's child;

No respect for themselves, our children gone wild.

Shooting and killing dying on the spot

I prayed, for the future, for the horror to stop.

Yes, I am afraid of the terror, that's within my times

Wars of a world, that wasn't even mine.

Where yesterday's deceptions were gainful lies.

Today's horrors are pies in the skies.

O' My Lord, I am so afraid of today's horrors

Please come, and change this world, before tomorrow.

My Soul is Afraid

The Ungrateful

Now the life of a sinner; I understand it not,

Their thoughtful ways are stumbling blocks.

I'm amazed they fight with ungodly tools,

with weapons of warfare, of ungrateful fools;

God gave us his Son, that we may see,

the grace and mercy that set us free.

God blessed me with power and good health,

and gave me the power to help myself.

But some reject, "The Christ" they don't know

Forgetting his love' running to and fro;

The ways of a sinner are stumbling blocks,

They see and they hear, and, they will not stop;

Knowing that the wages of sin, is always death'

Why don't men see, they can't help them self.

I am amazed how sin, is controlling most men,

Don't fast, don't pray, when they're at home,

Working in darkness, and they're all along.

Fighting with God with all their might;

Attempting to turn daytime into sinful night;

Hey, you ungrateful men, stop being such fools,

Obey God's commandments and his golden rules.

To love your neighbor, as you love yourself;

Love them with strong love, kindness, honesty and truth;

Please don't be 'The Ungrateful'.

Stolen from a Princess

In whoredom she glazed with flirtatious eyes,

In a wonderment of visions in living lies.

Her crown was decked with deceitful gold,

And an illusion came by and stole her soul.

She wore chains of love, trimmed in faith,

and bracelets of hope with rings of grace.

Stripped of her crown, called, boastful pride;

While standing in amazement, and loudly she cried;

The moment she understood her joy was gone

In a rage of madness, she yells "How wrong";

They capture her faith, tore it apart,

Ripped down her will, and then broke her heart;

But sweet knowledge, God gave her, that was so clear,

to understand, His commandments of being sincere.

And, the truthful crown, that was on her head,

Was also missing, someone has said.

Her rubies of works, her pearls of deeds,

was found to be void, as she cried on her knees.

And the pride we saw, that was in her eyes

she used for worship and praise.

She found repentance through it all,

And that's how the princess was saved.

God reconstructed my life

As, I wonder through Gods creation;

The Lord himself found me;

I was living my life in a state of sin.

Confounded I was, in this state of lies;

Conspiring with cunning fragments of deceptive sins;

Where in their County, their faith, stands for falsehood;

And the governor's was named, Sir Shame.

And the senator's last name was Mr. Do you want my Pain;

And, in the sickness of their mayor,

his efforts were perverted;

But daily, I walked down the avenues.

Of making the wrong decisions;

Standing on the corners of proud and disobedience.

Hanging out in the thoughts of accomplishing Fame;

Standing there dressed in ignorant,

with a pocket full of foolishness;

Giving myself over to an ungodly lifestyle;

But, when I prayed, "I CRIED-OUT"

Repentance came up fast.

True confession uttered sincerely from my heart.

A transformation occurred, a fire from heaven;

Filled me the more, standing on holy ground.

Thank you, O, Lord, for the lamb.

The City, The County, and The State of lies and deception

destroyed, in a moment time, all ungodliness fled;

And finally, I pull off all the garments of sinful living;

One by one departed they me.

Sorrow, shame, and pain were overcome, by faith.

God had reconstructed my life.

My Queen

To a God given princess, chose to be queen,

Let me be your prince, in the thoughts of your dream.

When you cry in your loneliness late at night,

I'll be there in your dreams, holding you tight.

Every moment, you'll find my thoughts are of you;

From the smelling of your perfume;

to sweet things you do.

O' king of my soul, lover of my queen;

Give us your blessings, to love with true means.

No lies, nor deceit, no ungodly show,

in faithfulness, we will walk, that our love may grow;

My Queen, My Queen, my princess I mean;

Declare to me your thoughts

and the truth of your dreams.

And O' the depths of my heart truly I do bring,

to my princess of beauty, soon to be, my Queen.

I will humble my heart, my heart, my heart,

and give you the love, your dreams have sought;

On tonight you will dream, my beautiful queen,

of ravishing thoughts, and on lovely things.

Your handsome prince will come in the night

will stand to protect you, and make thing alright,

And, when you awake, from your sleep,

to behold and see, that it's me.

That it not really a dream, but a reality;

From then on, we will build our love,

on a foundation of faith;

And build us our home, doing it God's way;

When I was There

When I was there

It made me so lonely I thought I would cry;

When, I looked into the eyes of their razor wires.

behind iron doors and concrete halls;

I was told to wait, while facing the walls;

It took months for reality to set in.

My life behind bars was about to begin.

I tell you the truth, my nerves were rattled;

We were packed in a cell (like herds of cattle)

or shall I say like it, did not matter.

Mt crime at the time was against the state;

Incarcerated for wrong, executed with hate.

And it challenged my mind, made me sit still,

It taught me respect, of who God really is.

A savior, a healer, a keeper of man:

A redeemer of souls, I couldn't understand.

When I was there

After awhile, I turned to Christ.

I didn't have to run, and I didn't have to fight.

Many a nights, I studied the word.

And finally, my brother, his word was heard.

When I was there

Nine months went by, I want to go home;

I'm afraid when I get there I'll be all along.

Finally When I was there

I learned to trust in Christ,

how to be strong in the power of his might.

And now that I'm out, I walk by faith, not by sight.

I believe in God, through our Lord Jesus Christ.

If walls could talk

If walls could talk, they would tell you some things

like the secret of secrets, done in the dark.

The hidden things they saw you do

when you lived in L-o-s-t Vegas, on Sinful Avenue;

The walls would tell, what things they knew,

revealing in detail, the ungodliness in you.

They would cry-loud and spare not, telling it all.

Then stand back, and watch, to see great men fall.

For their ungodly manners, right from the start;

The shameful things done in the dark

The private things that brings men tears

that's covered in darkness, and locked in fears.

If walls could talk, what would they tell?

Would they mix your lies and dirty details?

What you did in darkness, intending to hide

your sickness and madness, you masked and disguise.

If walls could talk, they would tell it all

The unadulterated truth, and shame us all.

With ears in the living room, roaming through the halls;

Painted in the dining room, and on bedroom walls;

If walls could talk, what would you do?

When the flax walls of darkness, start telling on you;

There's nowhere to run, and there's nowhere to hide.

And to those of us, living on the religious side,

But behind closed doors you'll find a wall;

Listening and waiting, and watching good men fall.

What if? Walls could talk, to tell on you?

I truly believe, they would obey God, and tell the truth

"If –walls- could- talk"

O'- My- God

You, O' my God" is a strong and mighty God

the most powerful creator of the universe;

Swift and sharp is thy Word

to cut away the evil fatness from one's soul,

O' My God, You know and discern the intent, of an evil heart'

(The evil mindset of thoughtful pride)

the evil that in sins, that so easily besets one's life.

Your Word is good; it does, do, and is still doing;

the impossible things, one could never do for himself.

O' My God, it was you, who sent your son; to redeem me

by dying on the cross for me

You it was, who tossed my sin, in the sea of forgetfulness.

Your son, "Jesus, The Christ", who showed me the way to obey;

O' My God, I am your creation, and you only shall I serve.

You gave me life, made me your wife, for life".

And, How much do I thank you; I truly, truly, thank you.

"Then I looked up"

And all the host heavens and earth, were rejoicing

and shouting, and giving God praises continually.

For my soul

"O'- My- God", O' my God, O'- My- God"

I must tell God

I confess, I must tell God how magnificent He is

For when I was living in my con-dem-nation;

Headed for my destruction, that's when God found me;

I must tell God, how grateful I am.

For, when I was there, there was no one else to help me.

God brought me out of the darkness,

into this marvel light.

I must tell God, how thankful I am.

For, when no one else could help.

He sent His son to set me free;

Who died for me, on Calvary;

Do you see I must tell God, how good He is

For, He leads me in his path of righteousness

He restored my soul.

He loves me so, He turned me around,

set my feet, on higher ground.

You see I have a reason that, I must tell God.

How wonderful He is for being my redeemer;

and my doctor, and my healer, and my lawyer.

I must continue to tell God, how much I love him.

By sacrificing the sacrifices of thanksgiving,

and declaring his works with rejoicing.

For He's been so good, and His mercy endureth forever.

I must continue to thank God, for saving my soul.

I have to tell God, "No, (I must tell God), (Thank You)

and Thank You, and thank you, and thankyouon.com"

A Wonderful, Wonderful Friend

Some men compromise their faith, with sinful hearts,

while others stand firm, in sinful smarts.

And if men would pull up, the pant of their minds;

they will understand then, the violence of their times.

If they let God intervene, where black lives matter;

they wouldn't look for guns, for neighborhood battles.

God will teach men then, on how to be smart'

to love one another, with a forgiving hearts;

They must bury all malice, where they tried to pretend,

to love one another, as wonderful friends;

God will show the advantages of a wonderful brother'

no lies, no killing, just loving one another.

With love and kindness the violence will stop.

The killing with words and shooting up the blocks.

We must trust our own hearts, and be not deceived;

We can be saved by Christ, if only we believe.

Then, and only then, we will find love and peace,

to stay from the madness, we see in the streets;

The lying will stop the corruption,

the killing will stop, the dying

and the world will become a better place,

because all soul matter to God:

Friends learns to be faithful and how to rely

on God's commandments, and how to apply.

God gave me a friend, A wonderful friend's friend.

He gave me His Son, O' How Wonderful

The End

PS: Ninety-nine point nine percent of the time,

Friends begin with Christ.

God Did It!

Image Credits

http://www.freeimages.com/photo/scriptures-1188105

http://www.freeimages.com/photo/anybody-listening-1563751

http://www.freeimages.com/photo/hands-1-1482489

http://www.freeimages.com/photo/praising-god-at-sunset-1503554

http://www.freeimages.com/photo/hands-of-god-2-1370509

http://www.freeimages.com/photo/praise-1576290

34961745R00063

Made in the USA
San Bernardino, CA
11 June 2016